THE BEST OF JIMI HENDRIX

ISBN 978-1-4234-6047-3

® Authentic Hendrix, LLC

EXPERIENCE

HENDRIX

"A JIMI HENDRIX FAMILY COMPANY"

EXCLUSIVELY DISTRIBUTED BY

HAL•LEONARD®
CORPORATION

7777 W. BLUEMOUND RD. P.O. BOX 13819 MILWAUKEE, WI 53213

Visit Hal Leonard Online at
www.halleonard.com

Visit EXPERIENCE HENDRIX Online at
www.jimi-hendrix.com

PURPLE HAZE

Words and Music by
JIMI HENDRIX

With a beat

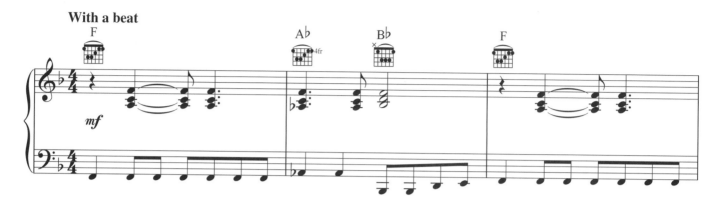

Pur-ple haze _____ all in my brain,

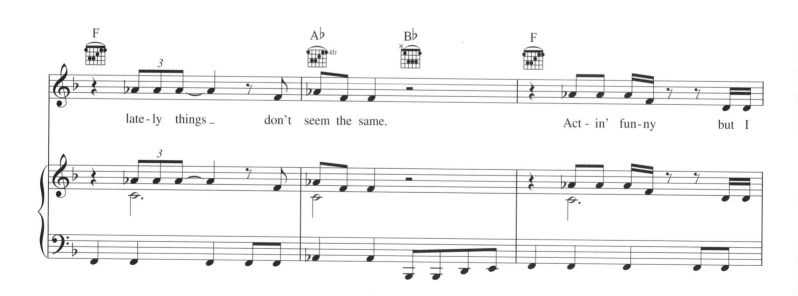

late-ly things _ don't seem the same.   Act-in' fun-ny   but I

FIRE

Words and Music by
JIMI HENDRIX

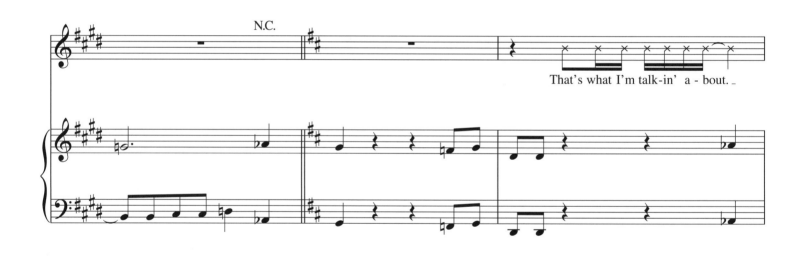

That's what I'm talk-in' a - bout.

Now dig this.   Ha!

THE WIND CRIES MARY

Words and Music by
JIMI HENDRIX

14

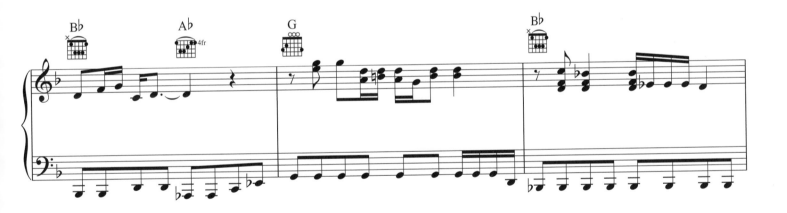

CROSSTOWN TRAFFIC

Words and Music by
JIMI HENDRIX

Do do do ____ do do do.

Do do do ____ do do.

HEY JOE

Words and Music by
BILLY ROBERTS

Hey, _____ Joe, ___ I said, where you gon-na run _____ to now? _____ Where you, where you gon-na go? Well, dig it. I'm go-in' way down south, _ way down _____ to Mex-i-co _____ way. ___ Al-right. _

ALL ALONG THE WATCHTOWER

Words and Music by
BOB DYLAN

Moderate Rock

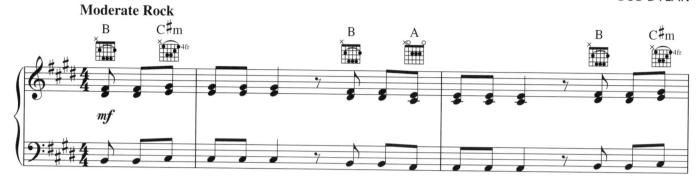

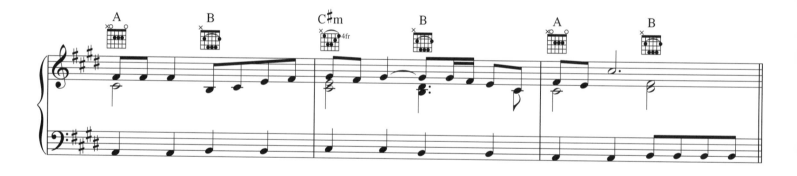

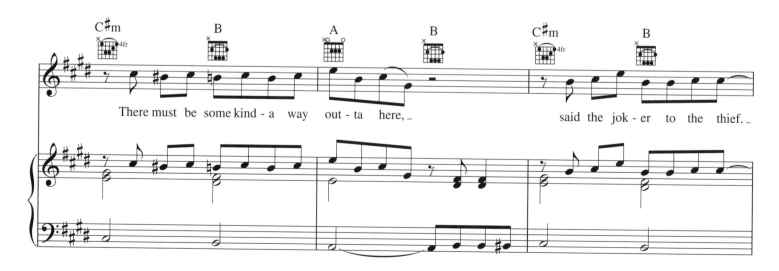

There must be some kind-a way out-ta here, _ said the jok-er to the thief. _

Repeat ad lib. and Fade

STONE FREE

Words and Music by
JIMI HENDRIX

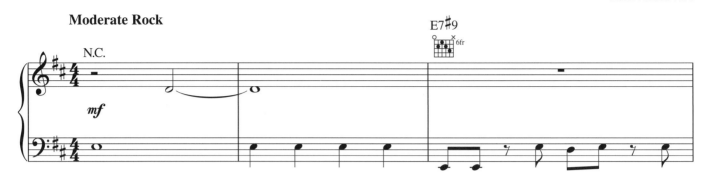

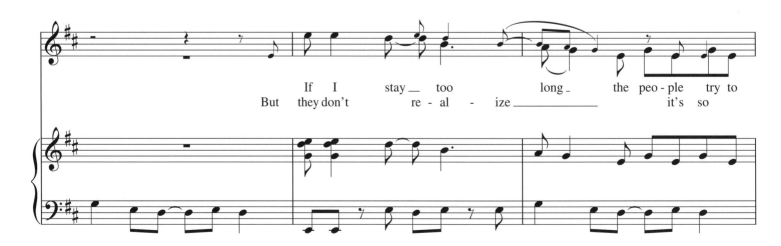

MANIC DEPRESSION

Words and Music by
JIMI HENDRIX

52

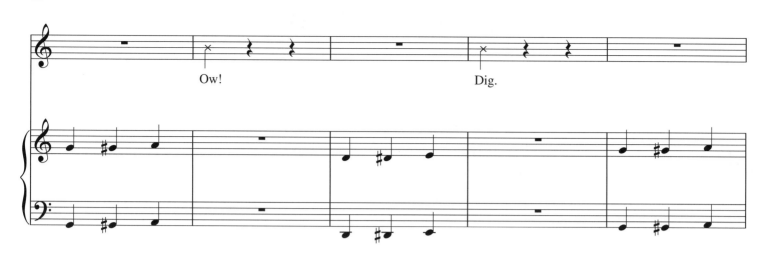

Ow!

Dig.

Ow!

1, 2

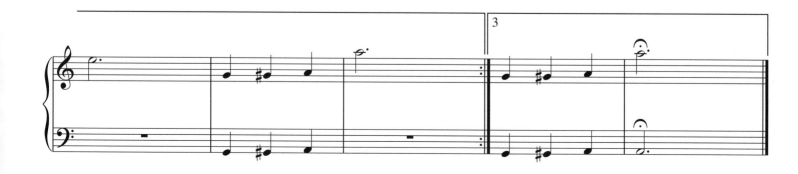

3

LITTLE WING

Words and Music by
JIMI HENDRIX

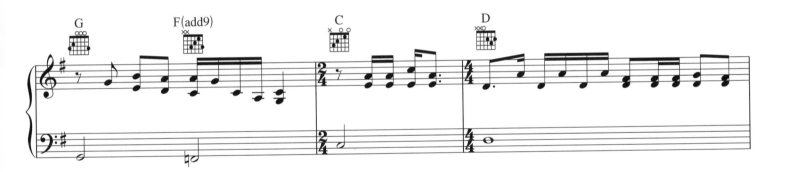

Well, she's walk-in'
Guitar solo ad lib.

through the clouds _____

with a

IF SIX WAS NINE

Words and Music by
JIMI HENDRIX

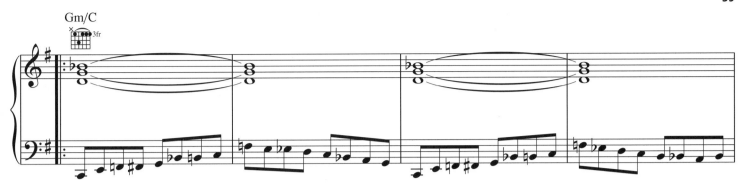

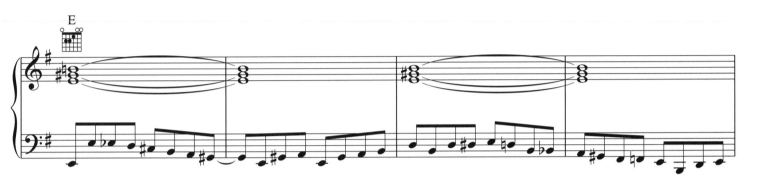

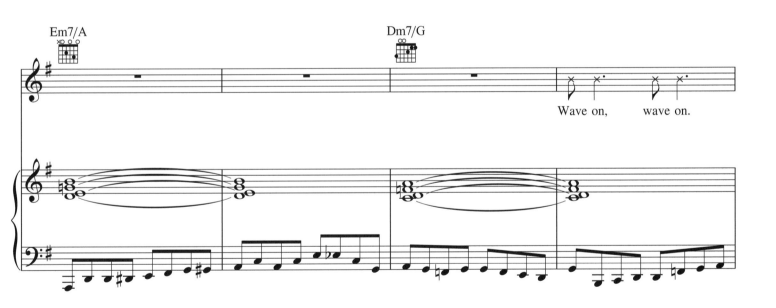

Wave on,   wave on.

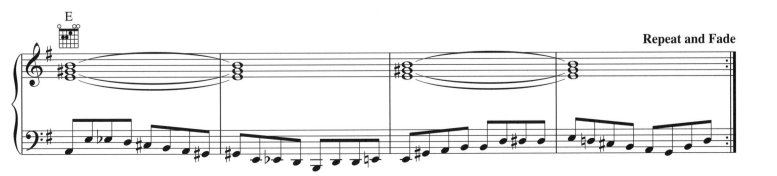

Repeat and Fade

FOXEY LADY

Words and Music by
JIMI HENDRIX

Moderate Rock

Em

Ooh, fox - ey la - dy, yeah, yeah. ___ You look so

good, ___ fox - ey. Oh, yeah, fox - ey, fox - ey.

Yeah, give us some, fox - ey. *You make me feel like sayin'*

Repeat and Fade

fox - ey, fox - ey. Fox - ey.

CASTLES MADE OF SAND

Words and Music by
JIMI HENDRIX

A lit - tle ven - tual - ly. _____

D.S. al Coda

There ___

CODA

ship is pass - ing my way."

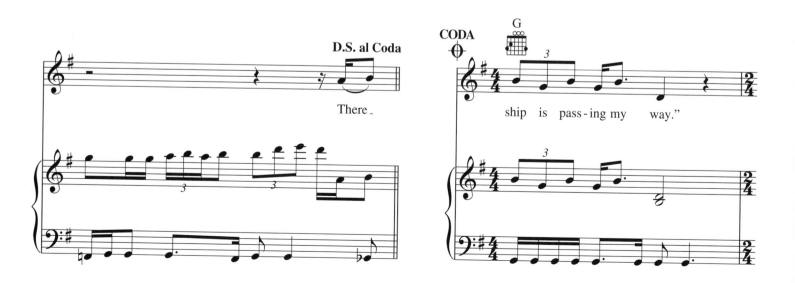

BOLD AS LOVE

Words and Music by
JIMI HENDRIX

*Guitarists: Tune down a half step.

I'm bold, ___ I'm bold as love, _____ yeah. _____

RED HOUSE

Words and Music by
JIMI HENDRIX

min-ute, some-thing's wrong here.
Instrumental

The key won't un-lock this door.

Wait a min-ute, some-thing's wrong.

Lord, have mer-cy, this key won't un-lock this

door.   Some-thing's go-ing wrong here.

I have a

VOODOO CHILD
(Slight Return)

Words and Music by
JIMI HENDRIX

Blues Rock

Recorded a half step lower.

84

Well, I stand up next to a moun-tain

and I chop it down ___ with the edge of my hand.

Yeah.

Well, I stand up next to a moun-tain

Lord knows I'm a voo - doo child, _ ba - by.

Guitar solo

Play 3 times

FREEDOM

Words and Music by
JIMI HENDRIX

She's right on, _____

straight a - head. ___ Straight a - head, __

NIGHT BIRD FLYING

Words and Music by
JIMI HENDRIX

ANGEL

Words and Music by
JIMI HENDRIX

DOLLY DAGGER

Words and Music by
JIMI HENDRIX

(Spoken:) "Oh, drink up, baby."

Bb7

Been rid - ing broom - sticks since she was fif - teen, __

Guitar solo

blow - in' out all __ the oth - er witch - es on __ the scene. __

She got a bull whip just as long as your life, __

this chick's gon-na turn you to a block of ice.___ Look out.

1

Here comes *End guitar solo* Yeah, look at

old burnt-out Su-per-man, try'n' to shoot his dust___ on the sun.___

2

Cap - tain Kar - ma kids, they're dead on the run.

Oh, words of love, do they ev - er touch Dol - ly Brown?

D.S. al Coda

Bet - ter get on some high - way and clear out of town. Here comes

CODA

Eb7   Bb7   F7   Bb7

She drinks the blood from the jag - ged edge.

Bet - ter watch out, ba - by. Here ___ comes your mas - ter. ___

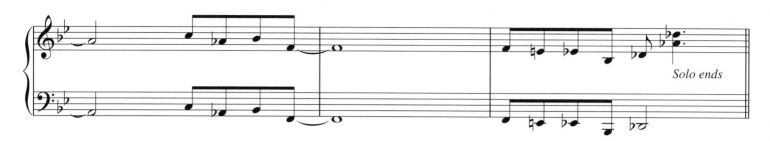

Solo ends

Bb7

Dol - ly, ___ heav - y ma - ma, ___ get it on, ___ get it on, ___

___ get it on. ___ Dol - ly, ___ heav - y ma - ma, ___

Optional Ending

Repeat ad lib. and Fade

get it on, ___ get it on, ___ get it on. ___

STAR SPANGLED BANNER
(Instrumental)

Adaptation by
JIMI HENDRIX

Freely

30 seconds of random guitar noises and effects

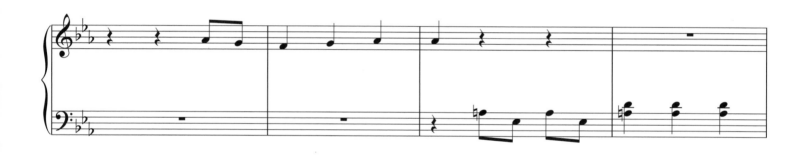

32 seconds of random guitar noises and effects

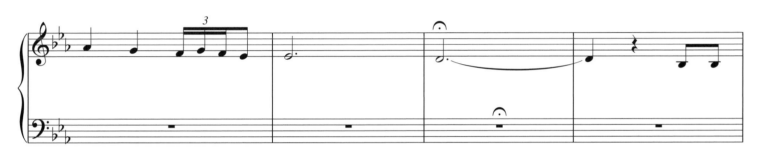

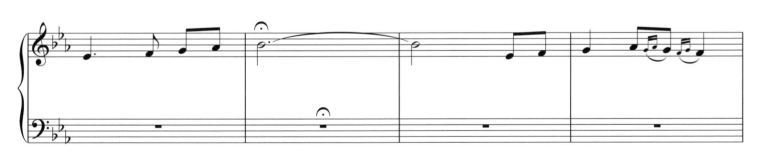

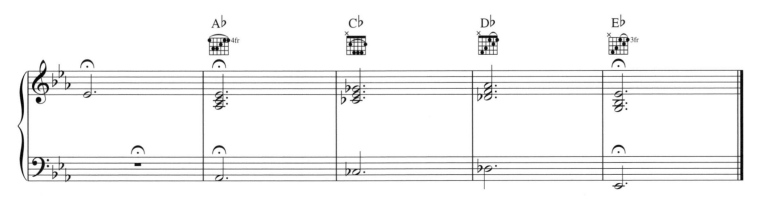